CONTENTS

Introduction

America's founding fathers believed that excessive involvement in foreign affairs was one sure method of endangering the ideals of liberty and freedom on which the country was founded. But despite their warnings to avoid "entangling alliances" and "monsters abroad," pursuing and protecting the national interests spawned by these lofty ideals has required increasingly complex interaction with other nations. As the country has grown into a global superpower, America's political and economic sphere of influence has come to include literally every corner of the world, and formulating effective foreign policy has become an important duty of this country's government. Indeed today, effective foreign policy is understood by most as a means of guaranteeing, rather than threatening, our way of life.

American foreign policy is influenced by many different factors--both directly and indirectly in many complicated and sometimes ambiguous ways. Although the primary responsibility for formulating and implementing foreign policy rests with presidential administrations, many aspects of our republican institutions and unique democracy shape US relations with other countries. First, the president shares with the Congress important foreign policy functions, such as control over foreign treaties and certain presidential appointments; another critical function, the power to officially declare war, is completely outside the president's authority. Second, concerns as diverse as the economy, public opinion, geography, ideology, and historical experience influence American policy toward its foreign partners, adversaries, and neighbors. Fortunately the US government has a long, and arguably successful, history of accounting for these factors in policy decisions. There are, however, factors with which today's policy makers have much less experience. One of these is international terrorism.

Violence, of the kind that fits contemporary definitions of international terrorism, is not new to the country[1]. Barbary pirates ravaged American shipping during Thomas Jefferson's administration. An anarchist killed President McKinley in 1901. Cuban rebels kidnapped US military personnel in 1958. And although terrorist attacks of every size and shape have since been unrelenting, America's vigilance and resolve in responding to these attacks, as reflected in clear and decisive action, has been considerably less impressive.

Concerns for the broader issues that usually surround terrorist acts have frequently served to mitigate a strong American response. Robert Kumamoto presents three such cases in his book, *International Terrorism and American Foreign Relations: 1945-1976*. Kumamoto analyzed the impact of international terrorism on US policy during the campaign of Jewish extremists against the British Mandatory Government in Palestine (1945-1948), the revolt of the Algerian nationalists against French rule (1954-1962), and the "Holy War" of the Palestinians against Israeli and American interests (1968-1976). He writes that "a historical analysis of these three cases reveals that, from an American perspective, international terrorism transcended the direct threat to lives and property and involved larger global concerns instead."[2] He concluded that in these cases the interconnection of terrorism with larger issues, such as the Cold War, Zionism, and Arab-Israeli tensions, forced the US to adopt a softer position than it would have preferred. While condemning the violent methods of terrorist groups, policy makers concluded that these wider US interests were best served by adopting policies of moderation, flexibility, and control rather than a strictly hard line approach against terrorism. As can be imagined, this method strained relations between the US and the British, French, and Israelis.

> [The] concern for the larger picture precluded strict adherence to hard-line
> policies and created, instead, an attitude of adaptability in the United States, both
> in Washington and amongst the American people. This also led, unfortunately, to
> tense relations with friends and foes who did not appreciate the reasons for

American restraint. Actions and policies based on moderation and flexibility were considered weak and vacillating....[3]

Today, the US does not suffer from "weak and vacillating" policies. But it has taken a stance against terrorism that may indeed strain relations with other countries, albeit for starkly different reasons than those above. In response to the historic attacks of September 11, the country has embarked on an unprecedented campaign--demonstrating the political will to use all instruments of its national power, unilaterally if necessary, against terrorists and their sponsors. President Bush described this campaign as a "war on terror...[that] will not end until every terrorist group of global reach has been found, stopped, and defeated."[4] Defeating *every* significant terrorist organization is an objective of immense scope. Prosecuting such a war would undoubtedly have important consequences for American foreign relations, potentially redefining US foreign policy for the early part of the new century.

Terrorism, then, has at times led the US towards "policies based on moderation and flexibility" and other times prompted radical leaps in policy. This paper studies the varying effects of international terrorism on US foreign policy. To that end, it is useful to first review the evolution of modern US counterterrorism policy and assess the character of the US response to terrorism. Then the effects of international terrorism on US foreign policy will be analyzed in each of three case studies--the bombing of the Marine barracks in Beirut, Lebanon in 1983, the attack on the La Belle Discoteque in West Germany in 1986, and the attacks on the World Trade Center and Pentagon in September 2001. This analysis will be used to draw lessons and make recommendations concerning US policy for the remainder of "America's New War."

Chapter One

US Counterterrorism Policy

The US government began keeping statistics concerning terrorist incidents in 1968. Since that time, terrorism has maintained its status as a problem worthy of a policy-- commanding various levels of importance and priority depending on the nature, effectiveness, and frequency of the latest attacks. This chapter will outline current US counterterrorism policy principles, explore the significant events and important arguments that have shaped the development of each, and provide an assessment of the character of the US response to terrorism.

There are four elements of current US counterterrorism policy:

- First, make no concessions to terrorists and strike no deals.
- Second, bring terrorists to justice for their crimes.
- Third, isolate and apply pressure on states that sponsor terrorism to force them to change their behavior.
- Fourth, bolster the counterterrorist capabilities of those countries that work with the United States and require assistance.[5]

The first principle developed from two simple ideas. First, negotiations would grant terrorist groups equal status with the government with which they negotiated; and second, concessions would encourage more violence. The history of this policy, however, reveals issues much more complex. Presumably to "preserve flexibility" and allow for concessions "if particular circumstances warranted," the State Department for a time resisted in making the policy public knowledge.[6] This may well have been a foreshadowing of official doubt concerning the practice, especially in light of well-known breaks with the policy and important arguments concerning its utility.

Examples of so-called breaks with the "no concessions" policy include meetings between the US government and the PLO in 1973, the return of Iranian funds by the US following the release of American hostages in 1980, and the Iran-Contra scandal of 1986. Interpretations of the meaning and consequences of the meetings between PLO representatives and the US deputy CIA director in late 1973 and early 1974 are mixed;[7] the serious effects of the latter incident are less so. In selling arms to Iran to support freedom fighters in Nicaragua, the Reagan administration not only violated US law, but also seriously undermined its "credibility in the international counterterrorism arena."[8]

There are also important arguments for and against a strict "no concessions" policy. One position holds that "[t]errorists are delighted even with limited concessions, for they have not only placed themselves on the state's level of authority, but then gained something demonstrable in the negotiations," and that "the state risks much in merely negotiating; to make concessions amounts to a double undermining of legitimate government."[9] Another view is that while the policy of no concessions has a convincingly "intuitive appeal", evidence does not support the claim that it contributes to the deterrence of terrorist acts. Supporters of this position explain that there are situations (both practical and moral) in which violations of the policy could be considered "reasonable", and therefore argues that "a more explicitly flexible version of the policy will be more useful."[10] This basic argument has existed as long as the policy itself, but the principle has nevertheless remained part of official US policy.

Treating terrorism as a criminal activity and focusing on bringing terrorists to justice was another of the early counter-terrorism policy decisions made by US officials. This policy principle dates from the 1970's and was developed to combat the kidnapping and hostage taking which to a large degree characterized the terrorism of the period. In differentiating between terrorist acts and the violence associated with social unrest or political struggles, the US consistently avoided discussions concerning definitions or causes of terrorism. American officials felt that these types of discussions diverted efforts from fighting terrorism toward resolving intractable political questions. Preferring to focus on individual terrorist acts rather than debate the legitimacy of a particular insurgency or discuss the root causes of terrorism, the government pursued international conventions and agreements designed to facilitate the capture and punishment of the individuals or groups committing terrorist acts.

The first successful applications of this policy principle can be traced to the Tokyo Agreement in 1963 and the Hague Convention in 1970. These United Nations (UN) efforts were intended to build cooperation on dealing with a specific contemporary problem--airplane hijackings. In 1971, the US attacked another emerging phenomenon, kidnapping incidents involving US officials in Latin America, by promoting the "Convention to Prevent and Punish Acts of Terrorism Taking the Form of Crimes Against Persons and Related Extortion that Are of International Significance" in the Organization of American States. As the terrorist threat has evolved, so have the conventions against it. There are now 12 UN Treaties against international terrorism that deal with issues ranging from "the seizure of aircraft to hostage taking to the financing of terrorism." Applying the rule of law through international agreements and domestic law remains a key component of US policy.

The third policy principle, isolating and applying pressure on state sponsors of terrorism, developed next as policy makers recognized the importance of state sponsorship. Although this type of support can be traced to Cuban activities in Central and Latin America after Castro's 1959 revolution, it did not affect US policy until economic sanctions became part of the US counterterrorism arsenal in the latter half of the 1970's. Counterterrorism policies had been designed to punish individuals, not governments, and diplomatic and economic sanctions were intended to fill that gap by focusing on the governments supporting the terrorists. One example, still in force today, is the 1979 Fenwick Amendment to the Export Administration Act that provided for the designation of state sponsors of terrorism and levied controls on the export of goods to those countries.[11] But 1979 was destined to usher in a more dramatic form of "pressure" for US counter-terrorism policy.

The Iranian seizure of the American embassy in Tehran revealed state sponsorship as an "unambiguous" tool of state and influenced the subsequent US recognition of state sponsorship as "a kind of warfare." Occurring during an election year, this event made dealing with state support of terrorism a high priority in the Reagan administration. And as his administration matured, a shift in terrorist tactics from hostage taking to bombings helped to set the stage for the use of military force as an acceptable method of applying pressure to state sponsors of terrorism.[12] Military operations against Libya in 1986, Iraq in 1993, and Afghanistan in 1998 and 2001 are evidence of the continued willingness of the US to use military, as well as political, diplomatic, and economic measures in applying pressure to state sponsors.

The final component of US counter-terrorism policy is to help countries who desire assistance in combating international terror. The State Department's Antiterrorism Assistance (ATA) Program, established in 1983, has trained more than 20,000 people from 100 countries in crisis management and various security skills.[13] Recent initiatives providing money, equipment, advisors, and intelligence to the Philippines, not to mention Pakistan, Afghanistan, and the Republic of Georgia demonstrate the continuing relevance of this policy to US counter-terrorism efforts.

As this brief history shows, the fundamental principles of today's counterterrorism policies have been in place for some time. These four policies have incrementally and necessarily expanded to meet the challenges of state sponsored terrorism and the adoption of more sophisticated and deadly methods of using terror, but have allowed for little practical emphasis on the underlying causes of terrorism. These four policies could be described as historically based, comprehensive, and necessarily focused. They could also be seen as legalistic, dogmatic, and narrowly focused. Subsequent events have certainly put a finer point on some of the elements, but the basic principles of the policy provide a common framework from which to evaluate the US experience with terrorism over the last 20 years.

Chapter Two

Lebanon

"Now is America's moment in the Middle East."
- Alexander Haig, Secretary of State, May 1982

American involvement in the Lebanese Civil War between June 1982 and February 1984 is remembered in many different ways. To the American armed forces, it may be remembered as an unfortunate period when an ill-defined mission and a vague threat merged to forever complicate military operations. To Israeli diplomats, it may be remembered as a time when the commitment of its most important ally was challenged. To the citizens of Lebanon, the period may have blurred with the countless others during which suffering, disappointment, and distrust were so commonplace. To international terrorists, it is surely remembered as an important victory over a world superpower.

When President Reagan first ordered the US Marines ashore in Beirut, Lebanon in 1982, he did so in support of the following policy principles: the withdrawal of all external forces from Lebanon; the establishment of a sovereign Lebanon with a strong central authority; and the security of Israel's northern border with Lebanon. When the Marines were withdrawn in 1984 as a result of a terrorist attack, these policies were seemingly abandoned and the crime went unpunished by US authorities. This chapter is not a detailed account of US involvement in Lebanon--although some background information will be presented. The purpose of this chapter is to explain how terrorism affected US policy in Lebanon in 1983.

Background

To say that Lebanon in 1982 was a country of many religious and political factions would be both an understatement and a crucial part of understanding the tragic history of this country. Division along religious and ethnic lines was not only a societal characteristic, but the very foundation on which governmental power was based. In 1920, the French established what is present-day Lebanon by combining Christian Mount Lebanon with the city of Beirut and the surrounding coastal areas where the Christians enjoyed only a slight majority over their Muslim countrymen. Under the French, Greater Lebanon developed into a prosperous republic. And although the economy thrived, the French stifled the political discontent that naturally arose from such a grouping.

After gaining independence in 1943, however, Lebanese politics were continually plagued by the troublesome Muslim-Christian divide. In response to this challenge, Christian and Muslim leaders developed an unwritten agreement called the National Pact, which established the following principles. First, Lebanese sovereignty would be safeguarded by prohibiting both Christian union with the West and a Muslim merger with the Arab world. The republic would at the same time, however, maintain its valuable commercial ties with the West and politically expedient neutrality among the Arab states. Lastly, major political officers would be selected according to the proportion of the principal sects in the general population. "This [system of government] [reflected] the recognition of the founders of independent Lebanon that sectarian cooperation was the key to the country's survival."[14]

But real political influence in Lebanon tended to be consolidated at the local, not the national, level. While local leaders were capable of joining forces to elect certain national figures, they also fiercely guarded their own spheres of influence against any strong central authority, including one of their own. This "localism" made the functioning of the Lebanese central government dependent on agreement among local leaders. When consensus could not be attained, especially between the major sects, the central government was absolutely powerless to act.[15]

The fragile balance characteristic of such a political system was beset by other disrupting dynamics. The wealth resulting from Lebanon's thriving commerce was unevenly distributed, with a clear preponderance in the hands of a small Christian-elite in Beirut. The natural tension resulting from this situation was aggravated by still another--the influx of thousands of Palestinians--from Palestine in 1948 and Jordan in 1970. Their presence had important consequences:

> Objectively, it upset the Christian-Moslem balance of power in favor of the Moslems. It offered not only a model to the radicalized Moslems but also a protective umbrella against Maronite high-handedness. It initiated a period of unprecedented tension between Lebanon and Israel. It mobilized the Palestinian refugee camp populations, exacerbating friction with their Maronite neighbors and the Lebanese authorities. It created a new era of explosive discord inside Lebanese society....[16]

As time progressed, the Palestinians became a powerful force outside the official political structure of the country, and their continued attacks into Israel across Lebanon's southern border exacerbated the polarization of Lebanese society--with the Christians generally opposing and the Muslims generally supporting the PLO. Additionally, in opposing the increasing PLO strength, many local leaders went their own way and even sought foreign assistance.[17] Unable to form a consensus at the national level, "the central government slowly weakened due to Christian feuds and rivalry, while discord between sects festered...[and the] immigrant Palestinian militias...became arrogant and demanding...."[18] The authority of the central government was destroyed, leaving each of the uncountable factions, each with its own militia, to vie for political control of the country. In August of 1975, this explosive atmosphere detonated, beginning Lebanon's Third Civil War.[19]

Lebanon quickly became a battleground for many foreign forces in addition to the several factions of Lebanese Christian, Muslims, and PLO fighters. Syria intervened almost immediately in order to improve its position vis-à-vis Israel. "The best way for Syria to come to terms with Israel was to establish a balance of power in Lebanon. To do so, Syria needed a stable and compliant regime in Lebanon and a subservient Palestinian movement under its leadership."[20] Fearing that the radical Palestinian fighters in Lebanon would prompt a war with Israel, Syria supported the Maronite Christian government, and other Christian militias, in an effort to counter the influence of the PLO. The desperate Christian militias welcomed this unlikely liaison as their only means of survival, while the PLO and other Muslim sects in Lebanon reacted angrily to the Syrian interference. Iraq and Libya supported surrogate forces fighting alongside the Palestinians in Lebanon in hopes of countering Syrian influence (and later, Israeli forces of occupation).[21]

There were many ceasefires and agreements over the next seven years, and plenty of negotiations, but no peace. In response to the increasing number of Palestinian attacks across its northern border, Israel invaded Lebanon in March 1978--establishing a ten-kilometer security zone inside Lebanese territory. In 1979 there were many Israeli raids into southern Lebanon as part of the policy of "constant harassment" of the Palestinian fighters in that region.[22] Under continuous threat from the Palestinians, and facing increased violence during the first half of 1982, Israel again invaded Lebanon in June of that year.

Originally advertised as a punitive expedition, the operation was described by the Israeli Cabinet as an effort to "place all civilian population of the Galilee beyond the range of the terrorist [Palestinian] fire."[23] Operation Peace for Galilee was designed to expel the PLO from southern Lebanon and reestablish a security zone inside Lebanon. But within three days, the invasion had progressed much farther than the required 40 kilometers, pushing all the way to Beirut and expanding to engage Syrian air and ground forces along the way. Linking up with

Christian militias in East Beirut, Israel laid seige to Muslim West Beirut. It appeared that Israel had decided to pursue a permanent solution to the PLO problem in Lebanon.

US Policy

Between 1945 and 1958, US Middle Eastern policies in general were aimed primarily at countering Soviet influence in the region, supporting stable Arab-Israeli relations, and ensuring the continued supply of Middle East oil to the Western world. American interests in Lebanon in particular were based on the Lebanese relationship to these larger issues. When in 1958 Lebanon's Second Civil War erupted as a result of endemic internal strife and deliberate external pressure from Syria and Egypt (designed to move Lebanon away from western ties and closer to the Arab sphere of influence), President Eisenhower dispatched US Marines to Beirut to restore order. Lebanon was the only Arab country in the Middle East subscribing to the Eisenhower Doctrine, and the President considered its political stability vital to US efforts to contain communism.[24]

In 1982, US interests were much the same. Like Eisenhower, President Reagan believed that unrest such as that in Lebanon was almost always the result of Soviet influence, and he viewed Israel as a "strategic partner" in the region.[25] Israel's security, then, was naturally an important US interest. It was in fact the US desire for the successful implementation of the Egypt-Israeli peace treaty and concerns over the wider Arab-Israeli conflict that initially drew the Reagan Administration's attention to Lebanon.[26]

Less than two weeks before the Israeli invasion, the US Secretary of State, Alexander Haig, identified the crisis in Lebanon as one of three issues that the US needed to address in the Middle East. He called Lebanon a "focal point of danger" and claimed that "the stability of the region hangs in the balance." He went on to say "the time has come to...take concerted action in support of Lebanon's territorial integrity…and …central government…."[27] The Reagan

Administration realized that Lebanon had once again become uniquely important to US interests.

The basic US policy goals in Lebanon were clearly articulated by President Reagan on 30

June 1982 and remained remarkably consistent throughout: a strong Lebanese central

government with effective control over all its territory; a secure southern border with Israel; and

the withdrawal of all foreign forces.[28] George Schultz replaced Haig as Secretary of State in July

1982 and became the chief architect of US policy in Lebanon and the Middle East, pursuing

these goals throughout Reagan's first term in office. Upon assuming his post, Schultz identified

the following objectives in support of the President's policy: to obtain a ceasefire among all

forces, to negotiate the departure of the PLO, to keep the Israeli Defense Force (IDF) out of

Beirut proper, to participate in an international military force requested by Lebanon, to gain the

withdrawal of all foreign forces from Lebanon, and to help Lebanon regain its sovereignty

throughout its territory.[29]

For the next 15 months, these objectives were pursued at the expense of torturous

negotiations, endless frustration, and immeasurable political capital. Schultz did achieve some

success with the PLO departure from Lebanon in August of 1982 and the May 17 Agreement in

1983 for the withdrawal of Israeli forces from Lebanon. But the PLO withdrawal did not

reduce the violence and the May 17 Agreement was dead-on-arrival due to Syrian intransigence.

Despite these setbacks, the Reagan Administration continued to expend time and resources in

support of a stable Lebanese government. The most visible evidence of that support was the US

contingent to the Multinational Force (MNF).

The MNF was in its second iteration in Beirut. Originally deployed in August 1982 to

assist the Lebanese Armed Forces (LAF) in providing a secure environment for the PLO evacuation, the force had been asked by the Lebanese government to return almost immediately. More violence and unrest followed the PLO's departure from Lebanon rather than the secure and peaceful environment envisaged. Within days of the PLO's departure, the new president-elect of Lebanon was assassinated, Israeli troops stormed into Beirut in anticipation of further unrest, and hundreds of unarmed Palestinians were massacred at the Sabra and Shatila refugee camps. These developments prompted the Lebanese to again request the MNF, and the US Marines returned in September of 1982.

The mission of the second MNF was to support the LAF in executing their duties in Beirut. American officials assumed that the various factions fighting in the city would view the US presence as neutral. But as the political and military situation developed, the US forces not only trained Lebanese government forces, but provided emergency ammunition resupply and naval gunfire support for Lebanese forces engaged in combat with some of these factions. These factions naturally viewed the MNF gradually not as a neutral force, but as an ally of the LAF, pro-Christian and anti-Muslim.[30]

As a result, the various factions increasingly targeted Marine positions in their assigned sector at the Beirut International Airport. As the violence escalated, the attacks shifted to other targets as well. In April of 1983, the US Embassy in Beirut was bombed and approximately 60 people were killed. And on October 23, 1983, a suicide bomber attacked the headquarters building of the Marine contingent of the MNF--killing 241 Marines.[31] The result of this last attack was dramatic for US policy in Lebanon and indeed in the Middle East. Four months after the attack, President Reagan ordered the withdrawal of the American contingent of the MNF.

Effects on US Policy

The most immediate and obvious effect on US policy was the withdrawal of the US Marines from the MNF and the loss of credibility, both in Lebanon and the entire Middle East, that this decision entailed. The complete collapse of support for the military presence is remarkable given that eleven days before the bombing Congress had approved, and the President had signed into law, a joint resolution which authorized US participation in the MNF for an additional 18 months. Further, President Reagan reiterated support for the MNF even six weeks after the attack, stating that the Marines would stay until "internal security is established and withdrawal of all forces is assured...."[32] By January 1984 however, support within the Congress and the administration had virtually disappeared--forcing the sudden and unilateral withdrawal of the American force even as the President stressed that US support of Lebanon was unshaken.

In February, President Reagan announced the withdrawal in a letter to Speaker of the House and the President pro tempore of the Senate, but he reiterated the long-held US policy goals in Lebanon. Characterizing the withdrawal as a redeployment to a more "defensible position", he said "U.S. foreign policy interests in Lebanon have not changed...."[33] The President also cited the "full and active" operation of the US Embassy in Beirut, the US military liaison teams still serving with the Lebanese Armed Forces, and the naval and air forces in the Mediterranean as signs of continuing US commitment.

But this did nothing to assuage the widespread perception that by removing the most convincing evidence of that commitment the US had indeed "cut and run." Secretary Schultz admitted in an interview in April 1984 that "there is a lack of credibility in pulling the forces out...and we have suffered a lot for that in the Middle East."[34] Indeed, most officials in the region recognized that when it came to Arab affairs, the Americans were chronically "short of breath." The Lebanese certainly realized that American support for their country was gone for all practical purposes.[35] "Henceforth Lebanon would be left primarily to the squabbles of its internal factions and its two powerful neighbors.'[36]

A second effect of the terrorist attack on US policy was the intermingling of Lebanese stability with the wider issue of Arab-Israeli peace. This was absolutely at odds with George Schultz' desire to keep these two policy objectives separated. He felt strongly that both initiatives must be pursued independently, and that "the peace process [should not be] made hostage to a restored stability in Lebanon....'[37] Shortly after assuming his post, he told the House Foreign Affairs Committee that "[t]he problems of Lebanon are distinct and must be addressed whenever possible separately from our Middle East peace initiative....'[38]

But Lebanese stability and Middle East peace were inextricably linked after the Beirut bombing. The day after the attack, Secretary Schultz wrote in a statement to Congress: "We are in Lebanon because the outcome in Lebanon will affect our position in the whole Middle East. To ask why Lebanon is important is to ask why the Middle East is important--because the answer is the same."[39] President Reagan confirmed this stance in a December address:

> Success in Lebanon is central to sustaining the broader peace process. We have
> vital interests in the Middle East which depend on peace and stability in that region.
> Indeed, the entire world has vital interests there. The region is central to the economic
> vitality of the Western world. If we fail in Lebanon, what happens to the prospects for
> peace, not just in Lebanon, but between Israel and her neighbors and in the entire Middle
> East?[40]

The interdependence of these issues was not a short-lived effect. Elie Salem, former Lebanese foreign minister and later informal adviser to the President of Lebanon, said that even in 1985, "the American officials I was dealing with talked about terrorism, and a resolution to the Palestinian problem. Only then, they hinted to me, could we proceed to solve the Lebanese problem."[41] Secretary Schultz' hopes of keeping Arab-Israeli peace and Lebanese stability separate as foreign relations issues was clearly a casualty of the terrorist attack.

A secondary effect of the policy intermingling was to prevent a firm response to the terrorist attack because of possible repercussions on wider issues. The US had a reasonable idea of who was responsible for the bombing, and even had a willing partner in the French, who had also suffered at the hands of the terrorists. But the US did not act. One reason was concern for civilian casualties and the inability to determine precisely those responsible. There was also the Weinberger-Schultz debate.

Secretary of State George Schultz and Secretary of Defense Casper Weinberger disagreed over the role of military force in combating terrorism. Weinberger believed that combat forces should be used only when, among other things, a vital national interest was clearly threatened and popular support for the action could "reasonably" be expected. He further required that force must be used only as a last resort and then in an overwhelming and decisive manner.[42] Schultz, on the other hand, felt that the measured application of military force would sometimes be an essential element of diplomacy. He thought it ludicrous that assurance of popular support should be sought in an emergency situation, and that [t]he idea that force should be used 'only as a last resort' means that, by the time of use, force is the *only* resort and likely a much more costly one than if used earlier."[43] This debate helped to paralyze US policy and prevented military retaliation in this case and others.

Next, in the aftermath of the bombing, the Reagan administration's interest in terrorism was dramatically raised--to the point that some authors have described it as an obsession.[44] There was definitely a growing realization and frustration within the administration that terrorism was going unpunished. Secretary Schultz believed that "[t]he hurried withdrawal of the [M]arines from Beirut ...left a clear message: terrorism works."[45] The implications of that self-indictment prompted Schultz to speak out forcefully on the subject beginning in April of 1984. His rhetoric gradually escalated to include advocating the position "that our responses [to terrorism] should go beyond passive defense to consider means of active prevention, preemption, and retaliation."[46] Policy makers in the Reagan Administration had used this kind of language before, following the Iranian hostage crisis. It was not widely accepted then, and prompted serious debate within the administration following the 1983 bombing.

Finally, following the bombing and the subsequent withdrawal, there was a significant lull in US Middle East peace efforts. There was no significant engagement by the US until early in 1988 following the uprising of the West Bank Palestinians, and even this engagement was at the urging of both Israel and Egypt.[47] And the only substantial talks in 1985 and 1986 were not undertaken on the initiative of the US but were prompted by Jordan. Certainly the 1984 elections and the Iran-Contra affair also contributed to this long lull, but the loss of credibility, the connection between Lebanese stability and US peace initiatives, and the increased focus on counterterrorism by the Reagan administration--all effects associated with the terrorist attack-- were important contributors as well.

This analysis indicates that the terrorist attack on the Marine barracks clearly had important effects on US foreign policy. The bombing caused support for the military presence to quickly collapse, resulting in the US withdrawal from the MNF and a subsequent loss of US credibility both in Lebanon and throughout the Middle East. In addition, the attack resulted in the intermingling of one policy objective, stability in Lebanon, with the wider issue of Middle East peace--contributing to the weak US response to the attack. Lastly, the attack precipitated an obsession with counterterrorism within the Reagan Administration and contributed to a significant lull in the Middle East peace process. The bombing of the Marine barracks in Beirut also marked the beginning of a "train of events" that changed counterterrorism policy in a dramatic way.

Chapter Three

Libya

"We Americans are slow to anger."

- Ronald Reagan, April 1986

It is hard to overstate the significance of the US experience with Libyan terrorism. Occurring in the aftermath of the US policy failures in Lebanon, America's forceful response to Libyan terrorism reversed a string of terrorist successes and made a lasting impression on both US policy makers, allies, and state sponsors of terror--at once liberating and complicating US counterterrorism policy. The successful military operation seemed to finally overcome the paralyzing Schultz-Weinberger debates concerning the use of force that had heretofore plagued the Reagan administration, but the operation also set an unfortunate precedent for future counterterrorism policy. The event which immediately preceded the attack, the terrorist bombing of the La Belle Discoteque in West Germany, was in reality just the last in a series of incidents involving Libyan support of terrorist attacks against US (and other foreign) civilian targets. This chapter will present some historical background, review US-Libyan relations prior to the attacks, and discuss the effects of Libyan terrorism on US foreign policy.

Background

Libya became an independent nation in 1951 after over three decades as an Italian colony. King Idris I, the first leader of independent Libya, became head of the federal monarchy ruling the largely agricultural and tribal society. Despite early competition for authority with the provincial leaders, Libya's newly formed central government maintained a relatively stable regime. King Idris' government developed a decidedly pro-Western foreign policy and became a conservative member of the Arab community. Libya provided military basing rights to both the

US and Great Britain in exchange for economic and military aid, and established diplomatic relations with France, Italy, Greece, Turkey, and the Soviet Union as well. These nations also provided various amounts of economic assistance (an offer from the Soviet Union was not accepted). Nevertheless, economic progress in Libya was painfully slow until the discovery of significant petroleum deposits in 1959.[48]

This event had important consequences for Libya. While obviously improving the economic health of the impoverished society, the management of this wealth helped to focus Libyan political attention on the "inefficient and cumbersome" nature of the federal system of government. As a result, King Idris abolished the federal system and established a unitary monarchy, thereby greatly increasing the power of the central government. While certainly benefiting from the stability offered by the strong central authority, Libyan citizens became dissatisfied with the corrupt and aloof bureaucracy and the grossly uneven distribution of wealth that developed. Concurrently, a growing anti-Western sentiment developed within the Libyan population--fueled by the Arab nationalism of Egypt's Gamal Nasser and the anti-Western reaction to the 1967 Arab-Israeli war. Reflecting this mood, the Libyan government requested the early withdrawal of British and American forces from their Libyan bases in 1966 and 1970 respectively. The failure of King Idris' government to gain the loyalty and trust of the general population further exacerbated the political unrest in Libya. These factors created the conditions under which Muammar Qaddafi came to power in 1969.[49]

Qaddafi's Revolutionary Command Council (RCC), as the new ruling body was called, espoused a strongly pan-Arab, pro-Palestinian, and vehemently anti-Israeli and anti-American stance. In domestic politics, Qaddafi challenged the Western oil companies and succeeded in obtaining concessions that dramatically increased Libyan oil revenues in the first years of his government. The redistribution of this additional income greatly enhanced the life of the general populace--raising personal income and improving education, medical care, and housing--and the standing of the new Libyan leader in the country and throughout the region.[50] But Qaddafi's early approval ratings did not last due to his ruinous economic policies and oppressive domestic practices.

Claiming to reject both capitalism and communism, Qaddafi instituted economic reforms that alienated the affluent of Libya by limiting personal wealth and turning over private businesses to the "workers' committees".[51] These practices led to widespread opposition and corruption as the upper classes circumvented the system to avoid personal losses. As industrial development and agricultural production fell predictably, Libya's economy became decidedly (and dangerously) dependent on oil revenue. And when oil revenues fell precipitously in the mid-1980's, the country's prosperity declined rapidly. The resulting shortages of food, housing, and other goods and services created resentment for Qaddafi's revolutionary practices, and as dissatisfaction with Qaddafi's regime grew, so did his oppressive practices.

Since the beginning of his reign, Qaddafi had been frustrated by the population's "lack of revolutionary fervor" in responding to his ideology. In addition to "revolutionary committees" and special intelligence services designed to bully and boost enthusiasm for his programs, he imprisoned, tortured, and killed political dissidents and imposed increasingly repressive social controls. Over time, Qaddafi alienated practically every segment of Libyan society. "In the 1980's, it was clear that, though helpless to oppose him, most Libyans had grown disenchanted with Qaddafi's rule."[52]

Qaddafi's foreign relations were equally unsettling. His major policy principles included Libyan expansionism, the promotion of Islam, Arab unity, fanatical dedication to the destruction of Israel, and unabashed hatred for the West. He annexed parts of Chad and Niger and aligned Libya with the Soviets in supporting leftist regimes throughout Africa. He made economic aid to other African nations contingent on their renunciation of Christianity, acceptance of Islamic practices, and opposition to Israel. He sought the leadership of the Arab world, and when his methods proved too radical for the other Arab leaders, he plotted to assassinate their leaders or otherwise subvert their governments. And finally, under Qaddafi's leadership, Libya became "the model of a state devoted to international terrorism." [53]

Libya has armed, financed, trained, and provided safe haven to terrorists all over the world since Qaddafi's rise to power. In the Middle East, Asia, Africa, and Europe, he or his diplomats have supported separatists, rebels, and mercenaries of every cause and persuasion-- with the Libyan leader sometimes directly involved in the planning of attacks. Libya was involved in the 1972 Munich Olympics massacre, the killings at the Athens and Rome airports in 1973, the Entebbe hijacking in 1976, and an assassination attempt on Anwar Sadat in 1980.[54] It was Qaddafi's propensity for terrorism that defined US-Libyan relations.

US Policy

Libya's destabilizing regional behavior and support of terrorism have undermined US-Libyan relations since the beginning of the Qaddafi reign. Despite early US attempts at maintaining good relations, America's support for Israel and the Middle East peace process made it a primary target of Libya's inflammatory rhetoric and terrorism. Qaddafi's early and consistent policy of sponsoring terrorist attacks on US citizens and property gradually transformed US policy from "conciliation toward Libya to...low key, low-priority opposition" as early as 1973.[55] Presidents Nixon, Ford, and Carter witnessed the steady deterioration of relations, with the Libyan opposition to the Camp David Accords and their open involvement in the Iranian hostage crisis representing significant obstacles during the latter administration. When Reagan assumed office in 1981 and announced that his administration would take "swift and effective retribution" against terrorist acts, the stage was seemingly set for an inevitable clash.

Tangible evidence of the dramatic action promised by Reagan's stark announcement was still several years and many Libyan transgressions away, but Reagan clearly favored a stronger policy toward Libya than his predecessor. Early in his administration, the desire to isolate Libya was evident. During the first half of 1981, in response to "Tripoli's support for international terrorism…, its expansionism in Africa, [and] its military relationship with the USSR…," the US expelled Libyan diplomats, increased military aid to Sudan, Morocco, and Tunisia, and authorized secret efforts to form and support opposition to Qaddafi's rule.[56]

More incidents followed. The US challenged Libya's claim to the Gulf of Sidra in 1981, resulting in the downing of two Libyan planes by the US Navy. Libyan threats against President Reagan followed. Libya publicly gloated over and probably provided support for Anwar Sadat's assassination. Relations continued to sour as the US announced a boycott on Libyan oil as well as other economic penalties in March 1982.

The US debacle in Lebanon at the hands of terrorists in October 1983 increased the public debate over the administration's response to terrorism but did not draw the "swift and effective retribution" promised in the early days of the Reagan administration. Perhaps encouraged by a perceived victory in Lebanon, Libyan provocation heated up again in 1984 and 1985 after a relative lull in 1982 and 1983.

Despite more tough US talk and a markedly more aggressive counterterrorism policy signed in April 1984, Qaddafi continued to support terrorist attacks against the US. His involvement in the Abu Nidal attacks at the Rome and Vienna airports in December 1985, during which five Americans were killed, prompted the Reagan administration to break all economic ties with Libya and declare that further Libyan sponsored attacks on US citizens abroad would be considered as attacks "by regular Libyan forces warranting necessary and proportionate acts of self-defense."[57] After further tensions in the Gulf of Sidra in March 1986, in which the US Navy sunk Libyan patrol boats and bombed radar sites, the US was finally prompted to action. In April, an explosion at the La Belle discotheque in West Berlin injured over two hundred people and killed two American soldiers. US intelligence revealed "unmistakable" Libyan involvement. Nine days later, US warplanes bombed military targets in Tripoli and Benghazi.[58]

Effects on US Policy

"The Libyan strikes…demonstrated that there can be situations in which the United States can use military force in the Middle East without catastrophic consequences for its interests."[59] While the US attacks on Libya did draw "intense international criticism," there was not irreparable damage to important US interests. While the majority of European countries opposed the use of force against Qaddafi, they also disapproved of his terrorism. Their most common reason for the opposition to military force was that such a response to terrorism would only cause more violence. This did not occur in the wake of the US attacks. In fact, after some immediate "revenge" attacks, terrorism in general (especially attacks emanating from notable state sponsors Libya and Syria) dropped markedly over the next 18 months.[60] There was also a belief among many Middle East scholars that such drastic measures would focus attention on Qaddafi and make him a hero in the Arab world. This did not happen either. And neither did important US foreign relations (US-Arab, US-European, US-Soviet) suffer any long-term damage as a result of the raid.[61] These developments helped to establish military force as a realistic and credible threat to terrorists and their sponsors.

Unfortunately, the newfound ability to use force brought with it the "smoking gun" requirement. That is, convincing evidence of state involvement in an act of terror was established as a necessary prerequisite for military retaliation.

By early 1987 the threshold of punishment appeared to be direct involvement of the sponsoring states in the actual perpetration of international terrorist attacks. The mere harboring, training, and arming of terrorist groups, on the other hand, were, according to the standards set by those western countries that are the main targets of these groups, manifestations of international conduct that however deplorable, did not justify a strong response. These criteria, in turn, undoubtedly determined the form of state-sponsored Middle Eastern terrorism to be expected in the near future.[62]

This criterion undoubtedly originated from the recognition of the need for both allied and public support for such a drastic response and remains a part of US policy. It was used in deciding to strike Iraq in 1993 and Afghanistan in 1998, as well as to refrain from retaliating after the attack on the USS Cole in 2000. The effect on policy was to limit the government's use of force options to isolated military strikes against specific terrorist targets instead of wider, or even preemptive, campaigns.

Despite this drawback, the US military action against Libya ushered in a new policy for the US. In explaining this to the American people immediately after the strikes, President Reagan said that "there should be no place on earth where terrorists can rest and train and practice their deadly skills." He further vowed that America "would act with others, if possible, and alone if necessary to ensure that terrorists have no sanctuary anywhere."[63] These words bear remarkable resemblance to another speech made 15 years later by another Republican president, after another terrorist incident again reshaped American foreign policy.

Chapter Four

911

"...and night fell on a different world."
- George W. Bush, September 2001

The physical destruction caused by the attacks on New York and Washington is rivaled only by the immense changes in America and American foreign relations since that time. There has arguably not been a time in US history when the focus of a presidential administration, indeed an entire nation, has changed so totally and so quickly. In response to the attacks, the US has launched a truly global war on terrorism, Phase I of which has focused on the al Qaeda terrorist network harbored by the Taliban regime in Afghanistan. But the war has not been limited to military operations nor to Afghanistan. It encompasses every conceivable front-- financial, intelligence, security, and diplomatic. The US has sent military advisors to the Philippines, Yemen, and the Republic of Georgia, frozen financial assets of suspected terrorist groups, and created a new Cabinet-level post to improve domestic security against future attacks. But most interestingly, on the diplomatic front, there are indications that many long-held foreign policy principles have fundamentally changed. It is no doubt too soon to distinguish between short-term differences--which can be expected after so momentous an event--and fundamental, long term shifts in foreign relations. Nevertheless, the purpose of this chapter is to explore these changes--and their possible consequences. But first, relevant portions of Afghan history, as well as America's pre-911 relations with Afghanistan and the Taliban regime, will be examined.

Background

Afghanistan is among the world's most tribal and fragmented societies. Strategically located between South, Central, and West Asia, the country bears the marks of all the great empires, cultures, and religions that have marked the history of the Asian continent. The Persian and Turkic Empires, Indian, European and Asian cultures, and the Hindu and Buddhist religions all have left their marks in various parts of this country at different times throughout its history. Since ancient times, great armies and migrating peoples have crossed and re-crossed this region, each planting seeds which have flowered into the multi-ethnic and multi-linguistic society which has been Afghanistan for hundreds of years. The "land of the Afghans" is today home to at least 21 distinct ethnic groups, representing approximately thirty different languages.

Afghanistan's unique geography also explains its second most prominent characteristic--that of a buffer state (and battleground) between powerful neighboring empires. In the sixteenth, seventeenth, and eighteenth centuries, both the Turkic empires to its north and the Persians to its west vied for control of Afghanistan and traveled through the country enroute to invasions of each other and India. In the nineteenth century, Afghanistan found itself caught in the "Great Game" between the expanding Russian and British Empires, "a clandestine war of wits and bribery and occasional military pressure as both powers kept each other at a respectable distance by maintaining Afghanistan as a buffer state between them."[64] Following World War II, Afghanistan played host to yet another "Great Game", played out against the backdrop of the 50-year ideological confrontation between the US and the Soviet Union known as the Cold War.

Afghanistan initially took advantage of its position by establishing ties with and accepting aid from both the US and the Soviet Union (incidentally, China was another important donor). But the Soviets gradually prevailed in this competition for influence, as the US policy of containment in the region took shape in the form of the Baghdad Pact, an anti-communist alliance which included Great Britain, Turkey, Iran, Iraq, and Afghanistan's arch rival, Pakistan. Although the US contributed over half a billion dollars in aid to Afghanistan between 1950 and 1979, Soviet contributions were quadruple that amount during the same period.[65] Predictably, along with the developmental aid came the USSR's increasingly significant influence and control over Afghanistan economics and politics as well. By 1973, when Mohammad Daoud seized power from King Zahir Shah and proclaimed Afghanistan a republic after over 200 years of monarchy, the country was well on its way to becoming a Soviet client state.

Daoud, like most of Afghanistan's tribes, was not a supporter of communism. His support for the Soviet partnership was based solely on the need for monetary and developmental support. But Daoud had seized power with the help of many leftist ideologues, and these elements became impatient with the pace of promised reforms. At about the same time, the Soviet Union became increasingly disappointed with Daoud's lack of cooperation and his western connections. In April 1978, the People's Democratic Party of Afghanistan (PDPA) overthrew Daoud's government in a bloody coup.

But the PDPA communists were hopelessly divided into two factions (the Khalqs and the Parchams) and were no more successful than Daoud in building a strong central authority. The regime's unpopular land and social reforms and clear dedication to communist principles at the expense of traditional Islamic customs provoked violent opposition from the conservative tribal groups making up the majority of the Afghan population. These revolts grew to include officers, soldiers, and entire units of the Afghan Army. As the Soviet Union's only southern ally, Afghanistan was extremely important to the Soviet's regional security--especially in light of the recent revolt in Iran. Accordingly, the Soviet Union was forced to increase its support to the PDPA even though the Soviet Union disapproved of many of their practices and policies and was painfully aware of their growing unpopularity. Despite this aid, the PDPA was unable to consolidate power or restore order within its own party, not to mention the general populace. In

December 1979, the Soviet Union invaded Afghanistan in an effort to put down the uprising and

maintain a pliable government in Kabul.

> Afghanistan [was thus] catapulted into the center of the intensified Cold War
> between the Soviet Union and the USA. The Afghan Mujaheddin were to become the
> US-backed, anti-Soviet shock troops. But for the Afghans the Soviet invasion was yet
> another attempt by outsiders to subdue them and replace their time-honoured religion and
> society with an alien ideology and social system. The jihad took on a new momentum as
> the USA, China, and Arab states poured in money and arms supplies to the Mujaheddin.
> Out of this conflict, which was to claim 1.5 million Afghan lives and only end when
> Soviet troops withdrew in 1989, would emerge a second generation of Mujaheddin who
> called themselves Taliban (or the students of Islam).[66]

US Policy

Following the Soviet withdrawal in 1989, US aid to Afghanistan dwindled as quickly as

the internal power struggles revived. True to its history, in the absence of an external threat, the

factions within Aghanistan turned on each other. The Mujaheddin overthrew the Soviet

sponsored Afghan President Najibullah, and the various factions fought each other to the

detriment and eventual destruction of central authority. It was through their ability to restore

order on a local, and eventually a national, level that the Taliban movement gained and

maintained power. But it was their decision to support terrorists (specifically Osama Bin Laden

and his al Qaeda network) that was most responsible for the US policy that brought about their

eventual demise.

Despite its lack of military and economic assistance, the US did have interests in the post-

Soviet Afghanistan. Primary among them was preventing Afghanistan from again becoming a

client of a regional power. The US specifically did not want Russia, Iran, or India to arm and

support proxy forces for the purpose of increasing their own influence within the war-torn

country. The extent to which the US supported the Taliban in the pursuit of this goal is not clear.[67] But by 1997, US policy had toward Afghanistan and the Taliban widened to include several other goals.

Several factors prompted this shift in US policy. First, the Clinton administration received considerable pressure from women's rights activists and other human rights groups concerning the Taliban's intolerant religious views and abhorrent record on women's rights. Second, the Taliban's export of drugs, terror, and radical fundamentalism was seen as a serious threat to Pakistan, a longtime ally and source of US leverage in the region. Third, and most significant, was the Taliban's refusal to close the terrorist training camps spread throughout Afghanistan and expel or extradite Osama Bin Laden.[68]

Bin Laden's anti-US rhetoric and threats became increasingly bothersome to the Clinton administration after credible evidence linked the 1993 World Trade Center bombers to Afghan training camps and implicated Bin Laden himself in the horrific bombings of the US embassies in Kenya and Tanzania in 1998. Following the embassy attacks, the Clinton administration "directed a campaign of increasing scope and lethality" against Bin Laden and al Qaeda. President Clinton expanded the covert actions to include the use of lethal force against Bin Laden and his lieutenants and even authorized attacks on the civilian aircraft that transported them. Clinton also stationed Navy submarines in waters nearby Afghanistan for prolonged periods of time to support short notice cruise missile launches--aborting several such attacks at the last minute due to the inability to confirm Bin Laden's location. Additionally, the administration supported several anti- Taliban forces and even sent a CIA team to survey airstrips and plant listening devices inside Afghanistan. And on at least two occasions during the last two years of his administration, Clinton sent senior representatives with a message to the Taliban that closely resembled President Bush's following the September 11th attacks: Bin Laden is

America's enemy, and that by refusing to turn him over, the Taliban was risking serious consequences. But the US never delivered. For despite these threats, US policy continued to exclude more decisive military actions, such as the use of ground forces, and prohibited expanding the fight to the Taliban regime that harbored Bin Laden. This policy was the administration's only feasible course of action, because in the words of his advisers, "the political and diplomatic market" would not support stronger measures. This policy was still being used by the Bush administration when the hijacked airliners crashed into the World Trade Center and Pentagon. [69]

Effects on US Policy

The first and most obvious effect of the attacks was to liberate US counterterrorism policy in much the same way as Libyan behavior in the 1980's helped George Schultz ultimately win his debate with Caspar Weinberger. The limitations under which US counterterrorism efforts operated prior to September 11 evaporated in the fireball that engulfed the Twin Towers. After the attacks, there were seemingly no limits. Within hours, the President announced what has come to be known as the Bush Doctrine: "We will make no distinction between the terrorists who committed these acts and those who harbor them."[70] And in his address to Congress nine days later, the President committed the nation collectively, and himself personally, to a lengthy campaign against worldwide terror and their sponsors, and a fundamental shift in the policy which had governed the American response to terrorism for so many years.

> We will direct every resource at our command, every means of diplomacy, every tool of intelligence, every instrument of law enforcement, every financial influence, and every necessary weapon of war, to the disruption and to the defeat of the global terror network....I will not forget this wound to our country and those who inflicted it. I will not yield; I will not rest; I will not relent in waging this struggle for freedom and security for the American people.[71]

The attacks also fundamentally changed the character of the Bush presidency. President Bush came to office with little experience, and maybe less interest, in foreign policy. Before the attacks, Bush policy makers focused on domestic issues such as cutting taxes and reforming education. Strengthening regional ties with Mexico and Canada and maintaining sanctions against Iraq may have been the top foreign policy concerns prior to September 11. The administration refused to join the Kyoto Protocol, promised to defend Taiwan, announced its intention to withdraw from the 1972 Antiballistic Missile Treaty and pull troops from the Balkans, and declined to lend meaningful support to solving the Palestinian-Israeli conflict. Although the administration was only eight months old, these policies indicated a strong tendency toward "selective disengagement" and unilateral action. The attacks dramatically shifted this focus as the Bush administration responded by "engaging with the world" in its war on terror and all but abandoning Mexico and regional concerns that did not pertain to the war.[72] Most notable among these changes were US relations with Russia, China, Pakistan/India, and its involvement with the Palestinian-Israeli conflict.

The case of Russia is among the most striking. Post-Cold War relations between the US and Russia never fulfilled their potential. For all the talk of a new world order, the two nations had not achieved the close constructive relationship many imagined possible. Differences over issues such as Russia's war in Chechnya and the Allied campaign in the Balkans had kept the Cold War-era rivalry alive. All that changed on September 11.

The Russian President, Vladimir Putin, was one of the first to speak with George Bush following the attacks. Putin expressed his condolences and canceled military exercises in a concrete example of Russian concern and support. In the months since that first call, the Bush administration has certainly tested that support in only the first phase of its new war. American troops and aircraft are along Russia's borders--inside Afghanistan and even former Soviet republics--for an as yet undetermined period of time. The US has also signaled its strong support for expanding NATO, an old Russian rival. And finally, Bush formally withdrew from the ABM Treaty, long seen by Russia as a key security agreement. Putin's restrained reaction to these developments served as the most convincing evidence of the new political environment that exists. The Russian president supported the military campaign in Afghanistan against the advice of his top military advisers, and despite disagreeing with the ABM decision, he said "that there would be no drama from Moscow."

But Putin's permissive approach has not been without cost. While showing the potential to reduce old tensions and spark new cooperation, the new relationship could also bring new problems. Senior Russian military commanders and the country's influential foreign policy elite see Putin's cooperation on ABM and the American military presence in Central Asia (not to mention the closure of an intelligence gathering base in Cuba) as huge concessions given with no commensurate return. "[Putin] has taken political arrows to the chest on strategic issues that boost Bush with his conservative base here. [But] there are now signs that the White House sees the huge political deficit Putin has been willing to run as ultimately unsustainable."[73]

In the hours following the attack, President Bush recognized the opportunity to improve relations around the world, specifically with Russia (and China).[74] His willingness to consider a decision-making role for Russia in an expanded NATO community, negotiations aimed at strategic arms reductions, and silence on Russia's military operations in Chechnya (once seen as an oppressive fight against separatists, not terrorists, with undue assaults of civilian lives and property) are clear evidence that he intends to help reduce Putin's "deficit". But if either Putin's or Bush's political capital is exhausted, the positions that he and Bush have staked out may well jeopardize future relations.

In many ways, US-Chinese relations prior to September 11 were similar to the state of affairs between Russia and the US. In fact, many experts felt that China and the US were headed for confrontation. The Chinese government opposed the abrogation of the ABM Treaty and resented America's criticism of their human rights record. The two governments were also at odds over what the US interpreted as protectionist Chinese trade practices, aggressive policies toward Taiwan, and indiscriminate arms sales. The standoff over China's delay in returning a downed American spy plane and its crew typifies the tension that existed between the two countries prior to the attacks in New York and Washington.

After September 11, each government's interest in these issues appears to have subsided, giving way to what may be the start of the "strategic partnership" envisioned by past administrations. Undoubtedly influenced by their own experience with terrorism, "China's leaders chose not to oppose American military action in Afghanistan, and even to support it in certain restricted ways."[75] China has shared military intelligence with the US and pledged $150 million for the reconstruction of Afghanistan--even though these operations are occurring in its strategic sphere of concern in Central Asia and the Philippines. China has also withheld comment on a new Japanese law allowing its military participation in the war. Chinese rhetoric concerning the ABM Treaty and Taiwan has cooled, and government officials have even stifled their disappointment that an important foreign policy initiative designed to increase its influence in Central Asia, the Shanghai Cooperation Organization (SCO), has been overshadowed by the war on terror.

Chinese cooperation in these matters is not, however, all good will. Indeed, some Chinese security analysts are already asking what China can expect in return for its unprecedented support of the war on terror.[76] It does appear that China is taking the opportunity to clamp down on many opposition groups (particularly those in Xinjiang) without establishing clear links to violent external organizations and using the America's war on terror to disguise its intolerance.[77] Additionally, before September 11 China's desire to increase its influence in Eurasia was evident in its Treaty of Good Neighborliness, Friendship and Cooperation with Russia signed two months before the WTC and Pentagon attacks. "Taken together, the formation of the SCO, coupled with the [Treaty of Good Neighborliness, Friendship and Cooperation], portend an important geopolitical transformation for Central Asia, Russia and China. These two regional giants are positioning themselves to define the rules under which the United States [and others] will be allowed to participate in the strategically important Central Asian region."[78] Chinese cooperation now may only be part of continuing efforts to strengthen its hand for the purpose of challenging US hegemony in the future. It may intend to call in these favors at an inopportune time for the US.

Equally as dramatic as the Russia and China cases is the change in the relationship between Pakistan and the US since September 11. Prior to the attacks, Pakistan's well-known and essential support of the Taliban regime, and confrontational relations with India, were a source of great irritation to US officials. At the urging of the US, Pakistan reversed course and supported the US-led war against the Taliban, and it restrained its reactions to new tensions with India caused by terrorist attacks. But this policy reversal is fraught with its own dangers. The war in Afghanistan is not popular with many of Pakistan's Pashtun population, and many others see the conciliatory stance with India as a sign of weakness. Depending on future events in the war on terror, these feelings could lead to significant unrest and problems for the Pakistani government--problems that the US may be held responsible for creating and may be obliged to solve.

Finally, another effect of the September 11 terrorist attack concerns the US policy on Israeli-Palestinian relations. In the early days of the Bush administration, there was a decided reluctance to become an active arbiter in the Middle East conflict, preferring instead to urge peace while remaining aloof from the process. There were also indications that Bush might endorse a Palestinian state, sending a subtle hint that the new administration might expect Israel to take the initiative in finding a solution to the impasse. Since the attacks, however, the administration has reversed course--firmly supporting Israel and threatening to sever ties with the Palestinian leader, Yasser Arafat, unless he is able to stop the terrorist attacks against the Israelis.[79] Such a stance may reduce America's ability to act as an honest broker in the Mideast crisis.

To say the least, the terrorists attacks of September 11 have had profound effects upon US foreign relations. The US has forged new partnerships and adopted new positions that would have been considered impossible or imprudent before. These changes may reflect wise policy decisions that will enhance long-term foreign relations, or they may turn out to be expensive roadblocks to future US interests. The next chapter lists several recommendations, based on lessons learned from the case studies analyzed in this paper, which may help to ensure that the relations that develop out of today's new political climate enhance American interests for a long time to come.

Chapter Five

Lessons and Recommendations

"Those who cannot remember the past are condemned to repeat it."
- George Santayana, *The Life of Reason*, 1905

Terrorism will not go away. Support for the global war on terror will. As evidenced throughout the last century, especially the last decade, the American people will not remain on a war footing any longer than the threat is readily apparent. And if terrorists remain true to their modus operandi, they will not attack again until the wounds of September 11th have healed. The same is true for international support. America enjoyed almost unconditional support for Phase I of its war but Phase II, inaugurated with the President's State of the Union Address, will be much more problematic. In that speech, President Bush labeled Iran, Iraq, and North Korea as an "axis of evil" and raised suspicions that they may be his next targets. This announcement did not meet with widespread approval.[80] In fact, despite his recent visit to Japan, South Korea, and China, the President has generated little support for an extension of the war beyond Afghanistan.[81] Beyond the problem of maintaining support for the fight against terrorism, there are other important historical lessons, suggested by the case studies covered in this paper, that are applicable to the remainder of "America's New War."

It is always somewhat dangerous to draw lessons from the past. More often than not, the lessons are not applicable to new situations because current conditions or factors are just different enough to render them unhelpful. This is not always recognized, and many so-called "lessons learned" are misapplied. But in this case, the similarities between the events are striking. The US experience in Lebanon, Libya, and Afghanistan all involved Republican presidents with little foreign policy experience following Democratic administrations remembered as being soft on terrorism. In each case, US military and diplomatic operations

39

were directed at a country characterized by a tribal society and a history of weak central authority. Additionally, in Lebanon, Libya, and Afghanistan, the US risked huge stakes in political capital while undergoing significant foreign policy changes. With those similarities in mind, the following lessons and recommendations are offered.

First and most importantly, America must maintain a strong presence in Afghanistan for the foreseeable future. After the experience in Beirut, where the US withdrawal was followed by a failure of American policy and a damaging loss in credibility throughout the region, this seems self-evident. But the US appears to be unwilling to lead that effort in Afghanistan, allowing Great Britain to assume the leadership of the peacekeeping force. The Bush administration should not hesitate to participate in nation building or peacekeeping. Afghanistan must be held up as the example of US capability, credibility, and resolve, not only for the benefit of current and future terrorists, but for our current and future partners as well. It may be melodramatic to claim that "Afghanistan is our new West Germany."[82] But the success of the remaining phases of the war on terror certainly depends in part on a stable, terror-free, Afghanistan; and only America has the financial and military capacity necessary to undertake such a task. Besides, it is not "Great Britain's war on terror;" it is America's. The US must take the lead in making Afghanistan a viable nation.[83]

Opponents of this position will rightfully assert that the US can not possibly afford to take on this level of commitment in every country that the war on terror touches. Further, critics will point out that the people of Afghanistan will interpret continued US involvement as an attempt to force a western-style government and culture on the Muslim nation. Similarly, others will say that regional powers will object to what they will surely see as a destabilizing spread of American influence.

So in order to avoid over commitment, the ability to assume such a level of responsibility should be weighed *before* taking action in another country on the scale of that taken in Afghanistan. Second, a long-term American presence does not necessarily mean a long-term military presence--as the security situation improves, diplomatic and financial support may suffice. Third, a stable government does not have to be democratic; it only has to eschew terrorism. America can protect and defend its interests in a foreign country without dominating the people, eradicating the culture, or intimidating the region.

Second, America must maintain an ability to discriminate between policy issues that are important, but separate, from the war on terror. That is, the US must avoid intermingling other important policy issues with its struggle against terrorism. This occurred despite attempts to avoid it in Lebanon in the 1980's, and US policy there as well as the wider issue of Mideast peace suffered greatly. Leaders in Lebanon have not forgotten how terrorists derailed American efforts to stabilize that country. Refusing to freeze the assets of some Palestinian groups that the US considers strictly terrorist organizations (Hamas), Rafic Hariri, the Lebanese Prime Minister, explained, "We are ready to cooperate on all the other things…, [b]ut everything related to the Arab-Israeli conflict has to be studied apart."[84]

In Phase II of its struggle against terrorism, issues such as Mideast peace, weapons proliferation, and human rights must not be inextricably tied to the wider conflict. These concerns are inherently important and, where logical, should be engaged independently of the new war. Also, foreign relations should not be based solely, or even primarily, on a nation's standing in the anti-terror coalition. China and Russia may still be "strategic competitors," and Syria and Libya may still be undeserving of our good will, regardless of their cooperation in the current campaign. During his recent visit to Asia, the President challenged China on their sales of missile technology while thanking them for their help in fighting terrorism. This is good policy. It is not good policy to "[refrain] from confronting [Syria] about its illicit imports of Iraqi oil [in hopes of nurturing] a growing intelligence relationship…in the war on terrorism…"[85]

In the same spirit, the US must overcome the emotion of September 11 and resist treating terrorism as its most important concern. It should vigorously pursue the Bush Doctrine and never revert to the neglect of the last decade, but must do so with the perspective that terrorism is "only one of many [threats] and not the most important."[86] Terrorism does not rise to the same threat level as a China-Russia coalition aimed at US interests, for example. This applies to domestic concerns as well. In a recent speech to the National Cattlemen's Beef Association, President Bush called farm subsidies a "national security issue." Making everything a national security concern serves to dilute, not strengthen the war against terror.

Third, the US must maintain the will to act preemptively and unilaterally against terrorists and their sponsors. American strikes in Libya signaled a significant policy shift in counterterrorism policy. The prerequisite of allied support based on sufficient evidence of involvement (the smoking gun) developed out of that experience as well, and hampered US actions for the next fifteen years. Seeking support from the international community is understandable and right, but the US must truly be prepared to take unilateral action in Phase II of its war to be successful. The experience in Libya demonstrated that military force, even with minimal allied support, can succeed in deterring terrorists (and their state sponsors) without alienating friends or driving enemies to retaliate. And the experience of the Clinton administration (and the early part of the Bush Presidency) taught that "America could never again fail to act when presented with a clear threat to its people." President Bush has commented that "[c]oalitions are all very well…but if necessary the United States [is] powerful enough to go it alone."[87] And in his State of the Union Address, the President indicated that preemptive action is indeed part of the Bush Doctrine. In the future, when strong action is again called for in the fight against terrorism, the US should not allow a lack of international support to impede its actions.

Lastly, the US must confront not just the terrorists and their sponsors, but the root causes of terrorism as well. America has long abhorred this argument.[88] But the fact that the country is still dealing with terrorism is proof that past and current policies are not enough. It is sensible that a comprehensive strategy against terrorism would include some level of effort aimed at the poverty, oppression, and other grievances that give rise to terror. And this can be done without "going soft" on terrorism. The US works to prevent future crime through education and social programs while simultaneously punishing today's criminals. In the same way, while relentlessly prosecuting its war on terror, America must also provide economic, diplomatic, and military support where required to prevent today's struggling (and cooperative) nations from becoming tomorrow's Afghanistans and Somalias. The administration's 2003 budget proposal is not encouraging in this respect. Money for peacekeeping and the support of new democracies, as well as economic aid for sub-Saharan Africa and Latin America, was cut by substantial amounts. "In the worst case, [these] numbers reflect skewed priorities that risk laying the groundwork for greater alienation--and yet another generation of extremists."[89] Of course, reducing the propagation of terror from one generation to the next is the ultimate purpose of the four recommendations outlined above.

In studying the various effects of terrorism on US foreign policy, the intent of the analysis presented in this paper was to glean lessons from America's past that may be useful in its continuing struggle against terrorism. Focusing on the attacks on the Marine Barracks in

Beirut in 1983, the La Belle Discoteque in West Germany in 1986, and the World Trade Center and Pentagon in 2001, the study concluded that terrorism has indeed had important effects on US policies. For example, terrorism in Lebanon contributed to a complete failure of US policy objectives, created a damaging link between stability in Lebanon and the wider issue of Middle East peace, and was a factor in the lack of effective American participation in the Middle East peace process between 1984 and 1988. Additionally, the American experience with Libyan terrorism, capped by the attack on the La Belle Discoteque in 1986, helped to first introduce military force as a realistic and credible counterterrorism policy option. And the historic attacks of September 11 not only fundamentally changed the character and focus of a presidential administration, but also altered the global foreign relations landscape in many complex ways-- most notably between the US and Russia, China, and Pakistan. Studying these effects led to the recommendations presented above.

Taken alone, none of the recommendations will be of much value in "America's New War." But if pursued as part of an integrated and sustained policy, international terrorism will certainly suffer. The question is, can America realistically pursue these policies? Can America keep the peace and build nations where necessary, effectively discriminate between issues that are terror-related and those that are not, act preemptively and unilaterally when required, and work to reduce the causes of terrorism at the same time? Certainly the nation that prevailed against the Nazis, rebuilt Europe, and outlasted the Communists can also win against the terrorists. But "[w]hat it requires of us--what it has abruptly demanded of the new Administration--is a broad-based and sometimes violent effort."[90] A balanced and multi-dimensional approach, suggested by the past 20 years' experience, will be the difference between haphazardly reacting to individual terrorist acts and effectively controlling terrorism over the long term.

Notes

[1] "Terrorism is the deliberate and systematic murder, maiming, and menacing of the innocent to inspire fear for political ends." Benjamin Netanyahu, "Defining Terrorism," in *Terrorism: How the West Can Win*, ed. Benjamin Netanyahu (New York: Farrar, Strauss, Giroux, 1986), 9. According to the State Department's definition, the term "innocent" includes "military personnel who at the time of the attack are unarmed or not on duty. Also [included are the] attacks on military installations or on armed military personnel when a state of military hostilities does not exist at the site." Department of State, *Patterns of Global Terrorism: 2000* (Washington, DC: GPO, 2001), Publication 10822, vi.

[2] Robert Kumamoto, *International Terrorism and American Foreign Relations: 1945-1976* (Boston, MA: Northeastern University Press, 1999), 8.

[3] Kumamoto, 198-199.

[4] George W. Bush, "Address to a Joint Session of Congress and the American People," remarks delivered to a Joint Session of Congress, Washington, DC, 20 September 2001, URL: www.whitehouse.gov/news/releases, accessed on 7 February 2002.

[5] DoS, *Patterns of Global Terrorism: 2000,* iii.

[6] David Tucker, *Skirmishes at the Edge of Empire: The United States and International Terrorism* (Westport, CT: Praeger Publishers, 1997), 9.

[7] There are differing opinions as to the importance and effect of these meetings on terrorism in general. Kissinger described them as exploratory and inconsequential. Tucker wrote that a "meeting with an official representative of the United States, especially with one from whose aura something more than a mere exchange of information could be spun, despite official U.S. explanations, was a gain for the PLO sufficient to make it promise to behave in return. In short..., the [meetings were] a concession to the PLO and a success for its strategy of terrorism, the first success of terrorism against an important U.S. policy initiative." Henry Kissinger, *Years of Upheaval* (Boston, MA: Little, Brown and Company, 1982), 627-629; Tucker, 11-12.

[8] Tucker, 42.

[9] Harmon, 239.

[10] Tucker, 80.

[11] Tucker, 16-17.

[12] Tucker, 23-24, 31.

[13] Raphael F. Perl, *Terrorism, the Future, and U.S. Foreign Policy* (CRS Issue Brief for Congress, IB95112), 11.

[14] Department of Defense, *Report of the DOD Commission on Beirut International Airport Terrorist Act, October 23, 1983* (Washington, DC: GPO, 1983), 26.

[15] DoD, *Report of Commission on Beirut International Airport Terrorist Act,* 26.

[16] Agnes G. Korbani, *U.S. Intervention in Lebanon, 1958 and 1982: Presidential Decisionmaking* (New York: Praeger Publishers, 1991), 14-15.

[17] DoD, *Report of Commission on Beirut International Airport Terrorist Act*, 27.

[18] Edgar O'Ballance, *Civil War in Lebanon, 1975-92* (New York: St. Martin's Press, Inc., 1998), ix.

[19] The First Lebanese Civil War was fought from 1858 to 1861 and the second in 1958.

[20] Korbani, 62.

[21] O'Ballance, 25, 132-133.

[22] O'Ballance, 89.

[23] Department of State, *American Foreign Policy: Current Documents, 1982* (Washington, DC: GPO, 1985), Publication 9415, 805.

[24] Korbani, 2-3, 30-33

[25] William B. Quandt, *Peace Process: American Diplomacy and the Arab-Israeli Conflict since 1967* (Washington, DC: The Brookings Institution, 1993), 340.

[26] Quandt, 341.

[27] DoS, *American Foreign Policy: Current Documents, 1982*, 733, 736.

[28] DoS, *American Foreign Policy: Current Documents, 1982*, 817.

[29] George Schultz, *Turmoil and Triumph: My Years as Secretary of State* (New York: Macmillan Publishing Company, 1993), 44.

[30] DoD, *Report of Commission on Beirut International Airport Terrorist Act*, 42-43.

[31] Also on 23 October, a suicide bomber killed 58 French soldiers of the MNF; and on 4 November, another suicide attack killed 61 at the Israeli headquarters in Tyre. It is widely believed that Iranian fundamentalists (Hezbollah) supported by Syria were responsible for all three attacks.

[32] Department of State, *American Foreign Policy: Current Documents, 1983* (Washington, DC: GPO, 1985), Publication 9441, 804.

[33] Department of State, *American Foreign Policy: Current Documents, 1984* (Washington, DC: GPO, 1986), Publication 9462, 587.

[34] DoS, *American Foreign Policy: Current Documents, 1984*, 588.

[35] Elie A. Salem, *Violence & Diplomacy in Lebanon* (London: I.B. Tauris & Co Ltd, 1995), 163.

[36] Quandt, 350.

[37] Schultz, 98.

[38] DoS, *American Foreign Policy: Current Documents, 1982*, 759.

[39] DoS, *American Foreign Policy: Current Documents, 1983*, 792.

[40] DoS, *American Foreign Policy: Current Documents, 1983*, 804.

[41] Salem, 187.

[42] Caspar Weinberger, *Fighting for Peace* (New York: Warner Books, 1990), 159-160. The Weinberger Doctrine, as it has come to called, lists six specific conditions that should be satisfied before combat forces are used. Secretary Weinberger detailed this doctrine in a speech at the National Press Club on 28 November 1984.

[43] Schultz, 650.

[44] Quandt, 356; Schultz, 651.

[45] Schultz, 644.

[46] Schultz, 648.

[47] Quandt, 364-365.

[48] This paragraph summarized from *Libya: A Country Study*, 4th ed., by LaVerle Berry and others, Foreign Research Division, Library of Congress, DA Pam. No. 550-85 (Washington, DC: GPO, 1989), 38-39.

[49] This paragraph summarized from *Libya: A Country Study*, 39-41.

[50] Brian L. Davis, *Qaddafi, Terrorism, and the Origins of the U.S. Attack on Libya* (New York: Praeger Publishers, 1990), 3-4.

[51] Qadaffi's views were set forth in three volumes of his *Green Book*--a "thin blend" of socialism and nationalism that described his "Third Universal Theory." Harmon, 10; Davis, 4-5.

[52] Davis, 7.

[53] This paragraph is summarized from Davis, 9-10, 21.

[54] Davis, 10-13. For details on the less well known attacks at the Rome and Athens airports in 1973, in which approximately a dozen Americans were killed, see Edward F. Mickolus, *Transnational Terrorism: A Chronology of Events 1968-1979* (Westport, CT: Greenwood Press, 1980), 402, 422-23.

[55] Davis, 35.

[56] Davis, 39-40.

[57] Schultz, 677.

[58] In 1988, Libya was implicated in the bombing of Pan Am flight 103, which killed 270 (including 189 Americans). After years of being "ostracized and presiding over a country suffering economically," Qaddafi turned over two Libyan suspects in the Pan Am attack in 1999 in exchange for talks aimed at removing the economic sanctions imposed in 1986. The Clinton administration insisted that Libya take responsibility for the 1988 attack and compensate the families of the victims. Libya did not comply. Since September 11, there have been renewed efforts by Libya to shed its "pariah status" and end the economic sanctions. Qaddafi's government condemned the attacks as "horrifying, destructive" and has since provided intelligence in support of America's war on terror. But Libya remains on the State Department's list of state sponsors of terrorism and is still subject to the US sanctions (separate UN sanctions were lifted following the decision to hand over the Pan Am suspects). Robert S. Greenberger, "Sept. 11 Aids Gadhafi In Effort to Get Libya Off U.S. Terrorist List," *Wall Street Journal,* 14 January 2002, A1; Peter Slevin, "Bush White House Reconsidering Reagan's 'Evil Man,'" *Washington Post,* 11 March 2002, A14.

[59] Davis, 169.

[60] Davis, 166-167.

[61] Davis, 147, 150, 160-161.

[62] Ariel Merari, et al., *Inter 86: A Review of International Terrorism in 1986* (Boulder, CO: Westview, 1987), 34-35, quoted in Davis, 171.

[63] Department of State, *American Foreign Policy: Current Documents, 1986* (Washington, DC: GPO, 1987), Publication 9620, 451.

[64] Ahmed Rashid, *Taliban: Militant Islam, Oil, and Fundamentalism in Central Asia* (New Haven, London: Yale University Press, 2000), 11.

[65] Most of the US aid came in the 1950's, "after which Washington lost interest." Rashid, 13.

[66] Rashid, 13.

[67] Both Saudi Arabia and Pakistan were early supporters of the Taliban, and the US did not initially oppose this support. Some see this as evidence of at least tacit US support for the Taliban prior to that regime's open support of terrorism. Others claim that the US supported the Taliban in order to reduce Iranian and Russian influence in Afghanistan, among other reasons; and some US officials deny that the US supported the regime at any time. Rashid, 178-180; Kamal Mantinuddin, *The Taliban Phenomenon, Afghanistan 1994-1997* (UK: Oxford University Press, 1999), 161-163.

[68] Mantinuddin, 166-168; Rashid, 180-182.

[69] Barton Gellman, "Broad Effort Launched After '98 Attacks," *Washington Post*, 19 December 2001, A1.

[70] Dan Balz and Bob Woodward, "America's Chaotic Road to War," *Washington Post*, 27 January 2002, A13.

[71] George W. Bush, "Address to a Joint Session of Congress and the American People," 20 September 2001.

[72] Robin Wright and Doyle McManus, "Attacks Redefined Bush Foreign Policy," *Los Angeles Times,* 7 January 2002, A1.

[73] Jim Hoagland, "Strategic Odd Couple," *Washington Post,* 3 February 2002.

[74] Dan Balz and Bob Woodward, "America's Chaotic Road to War," *Washington Post*, 27 January 2002, A1.

[75] Aaron L. Friedberg, "Terror Aside, U.S. and China Remain Far Apart," *Wall Street Journal,* 20 February 2002. This writer goes on to say that in supporting US efforts in Afghanistan, "[t]he Chinese government [hoped] that the elimination of a nearby terrorist safe haven [would] help to constrict support for Islamist forces that it [accused] of waging guerrilla warfare in its western provinces." Much has been written concerning the legitimacy of China's counterterrorism policies, most of which centers on the Uighur separatists in the western province of Xinjiang. Most writers acknowledge the legitimate concern that China and all the other Central Asian nations have over the spread of Islamic extremism throughout their region, but claim that China is using the global war on terror as a cover to more effectively repress even peaceful political activists and religious movements all over China. In addition to this article, see also "Messages for Asia," editorial, *Washington Post*, 16 February 2002, A24, for a similar and representative presentation of this sentiment.

[76] John Pomfret, "China Sees Interests Tied to U.S.," *Washington Post*, 2 February 2002, A18.

[77] Friedberg, "Terror Aside," and "Messages for Asia," editorial, *Washington Post,* 16 February 2002, A24.

[78] Ariel Cohen, "U.S. Interests in Central Asia," testimony before the Subcommittee on Operations and Human Rights (IOHR) and the Subcommittee on Middle East and South Asia (MESA) House International Relations Committee, Washington, DC, 18 July 2001, URL: www.heritage.org/library/testimony, accessed 17 January 2002.

[79] The President did not break ties with Arafat because his advisers felt that would create a dangerous power vacuum and undermine Arab support for America's terrorism war. The President did, however, announce that no new efforts to broker Mideast peace would be undertaken until Arafat shows significant progress in reducing the attacks against Israel. Karen DeYoung, "Bush: U.S. Won't Cut Off Arafat," *Washington Post,* 2 February 2002, A1.

[80] The majority of European and Asian reaction to the President's speech has ranged from lukewarm to negative. "French Foreign Minister Hubert Vedrine has called President Bush's [strategy] 'simplistic.' German Foreign Minister Joschka Fischer said the U.S. was treating Europeans like 'satellites.' And the normally sensible European Foreign Affairs Commissioner Chris Patten called Mr. Bush's approach 'absolutist' and unilateralist overdrive.'" In general, the Asian reaction has been less critical but nevertheless leaders there were "dismayed by Bush's speech and warned about 'unnecessary tensions or escalation of rhetoric.'" R. James Wooley, "Where's the Posse?," *Wall Street Journal,* 25 February 2002; Peter Slevin and Mike Allen, "Bush's Asia Trip Will Focus on Terrorism," *Washington Post,* 16 February 2002.

[81] "While [the leaders of these countries] voiced unequivocal support for Mr. Bush's antiterrorism campaign in Afghanistan, Mr. Bush will return having made little progress lining up support for a broader war." On a similar mission in the Middle East, Vice President Cheney was equally unsuccessful in enlisting support for military action against Iraq. "[A]fter meeting with nine Arab leaders, the vice president conceded the region was 'preoccupied' by the violence [between the Israelis and Palestinians]...." Jordan's King Abdullah II explained in a response typical of leaders throughout the region: "'To attack Baghdad now would be a disaster. ...the Middle East cannot support two wars at the same time--the Israeli-Palestinian conflict and an American intervention against Iraq.'" Former Secretary of State Henry Kissinger has written that such support is absolutely vital to a successful campaign against Iraq, and

"that [p]hase II [of the war on terror] is likely to separate those members of the coalition that joined so as to have veto power over American actions from those that are willing to [faithfully pursue the Bush Doctrine]." Jim VandeHei and Charles Hutzler, "Bush's China Visit Shows Antiterror Campaign Is Tough Sell," *Wall Street Journal,* 22 February 2002; Jeanne Cummings, "Arafat Nudges Iraq Off Cheney's Agenda," *Wall Street Journal,* 20 March 2002; Henry Kissinger, "Phase II and Iraq," *Washington Post,* 13 January 2002.

[82] Michael McFaul, "The Other Half of the Job," *Washington Post,* 5 February 2002

[83] Of course, there are many opponents of long-term involvement in Afghanistan. A common argument against such a policy is that Afghanistan's history highlights two clear roadblocks to US success: First, the difficulty (maybe impossibility) of forming a central government in Afghanistan capable of maintaining the support of the fragmented society, and second, the propensity of the Afghan people for violent opposition to *any* sustained foreign presence. Critics also claim that Americans have likewise demonstrated a traditional aversion to such open-ended commitments, and they cite the Vietnam experience as an example of the likely outcome of American efforts to stabilize Afghanistan. Others fear that US forces would be lucrative targets for any number of anti-Western groups. And finally, the inevitable failure would come at an immense cost in American money, prestige, and military power.

[84] Yaroslav Trofimov, "Brandishing Weapons and Aid, Hezbollah Tests U.S. Resolve," *Wall Street Journal,* 17 December 2001.

[85] Alan Sipress and Colum Lynch, "U.S. Avoids Confronting Syrians on Iraqi Oil," *Washington Post,* 14 February 2002, A1.

[86] Tucker, 49.

[87] "We Must Realise Bush Meant What He Said: This Is War," editorial, *London Daily Telegraph,* 7 February 2002.

[88] Secretary Schultz wrote, "Do poverty and injustice cause terrorism? We should work for social betterment but not legitimize terrorism in the meantime. Does political oppression cause terrorism? We should work for human rights and diplomatic solutions to conflicts.... In my firm view, people who engage in terror do not want peace or justice, and people who want peace and justice do not engage in terror.... Nothing [is] more odious or dangerous, in my view, than the line of argument that 'root causes' justify and legitimize terrorist acts." Schultz, 645-646, 676. American policy then, and since, has clearly focused more on punitive actions than on "social betterment."

[89] Robin Wright, "Don't Just Fund the War, Shell Out for Peace," *Washington Post,* 10 March 2002.

[90] Christopher C. Harmon, speech presented at the Secretary's Open Forum, Department of State, Washington, DC, 22 October 2001.

Bibliography

Davis, Brian L. *Qaddafi, Terrorism, and the Origins of the U.S. Attack on Libya.* New York: Praeger Publishers, 1990.

Department of Defense. *Report of the DOD Commission on Beirut International Airport Terrorist Act, October 23, 1983.* Washington, DC: GPO, 1983.

Department of State. *Patterns of Global Terrorism: 2000.* Washington, DC: GPO, 2001. Publication 10822.

Department of State. *American Foreign Policy: Current Documents, 1982.* Washington, DC: GPO, 1985. Publication 9415.

Department of State. *American Foreign Policy: Current Documents, 1983.* Washington, DC: GPO, 1985. Publication 9441.

Department of State. *American Foreign Policy: Current Documents, 1984.* Washington, DC: GPO, 1986. Publication 9462.

Harmon, Christopher C. *Terrorism Today.* Portland, OR: Frank Cass Publishers, 2000.

Haass, Richard N. *The Reluctant Sheriff: The United States After the Cold War.* New York: Council on Foreign Relations, Inc., 1997.

Kissinger, Henry. *Years of Upheaval.* Boston, MA: Little, Brown and Company, 1982.

Korbani, Agnes G. *U.S. Intervention in Lebanon, 1958 and 1982: Presidential Decisionmaking.* New York: Praeger Publishers, 1991.

Kumamoto, Robert. *International Terrorism and American Foreign Relations: 1945-1976* Boston, MA: Northeastern University Press, 1999.

Mantinuddin, Kamal. *The Taliban Phenomenon, Afghanistan 1994-1997.* UK: Oxford University Press, 1999.

Martin, David C. and Walcott, John. *Best Laid Plans: The Inside Story of America's War Against Terrorism.* New York: Harper and Row, Publishers, 1988.

McDougall, Walter A. *Promised Land, Crusader State: The American Encounter with the World Since 1776.* Boston, MA: Houghton Mifflin Company, 1997.

Mickolus, Edward F. *Transnational Terrorism: A Chronology of Events 1968-1979.* Westport, CT: Greenwood Press, 1980.

O'Ballance, Edgar. *Civil War in Lebanon, 1975-92.* New York: St. Martin's Press, Inc., 1998.

Pillar, Paul R. *Terrorism and U.S. Foreign Policy.* Washington, DC: Brookings Institution Press, 2001.

Quandt, William B. *Peace Process: American Diplomacy and the Arab-Israeli Conflict since 1967.* Washington, DC: The Brookings Institution, 1993.

Rashid, Ahmed. *Taliban: Militant Islam, Oil, and Fundamentalism in Central Asia.* New Haven, London: Yale University Press, 2000.

Salem, Elie A. *Violence & Diplomacy in Lebanon.* London: I.B. Tauris & Co Ltd, 1995.

Schultz, George. *Turmoil and Triumph: My Years as Secretary of State.* New York: Macmillan Publishing Company, 1993.

Terrorism: How the West Can Win. Ed. Benjamin Netanyahu. New York: Farrar, Strauss, Giroux. 1986.

Tucker, David. *Skirmishers at the Edge of Empire: The United States and International Terrorism.* Westport, CT: Praeger Publishers, 1997.

Washington Post, 19 December 2001; 13, 27 January 2002; 2-3, 5, 14, 16 February 2002; 10-11 March 2002.

Wall Street Journal, 17 December 2001; 14 January 2002; 20, 22, 25 February 2002; 20 March 2002.

"We Must Realise Bush Meant What He Said: This Is War." Editorial. *London Daily Telegraph*, 7 February 2002.

Weinberger, Caspar. *Fighting for Peace.* New York: Warner Books, 1990.

Wright, Robin and McManus, Doyle. "Attacks Redefined Bush Foreign Policy." *Los Angeles Times*, 7 January 2002, A1.